Life's Challenges!

THE NIGHT DAD
WENT TO PRISON

What to expect when someone
you love goes to prison

by Melissa Higgins

illustrated by
Wednesday Kirwan

raintree
a Capstone company — publishers for children

9112000291941

D0589731

This is one of my *before* drawings. *Before* means "before my dad went to prison." Dad and I didn't catch anything, but we had fun anyway.

My dad calls me Sketch because I like to draw. Miss Sanchez, my school counsellor, says drawing is a good way for me to show my feelings. I must have a lot of feelings. I draw all the time!

2

We were at Dad's flat the night the police came. Lights flashed. Neighbours stared. The police officers put my dad in handcuffs. Jasmine and TJ started crying.

One of the officers walked over to us. I thought he was going to arrest us too! But he smiled and handed TJ a teddy bear.

"Where are you taking my dad?" I asked. "What has he done?"

"Your dad may have broken a law," the officer said. "We need to ask him some questions at the police station."

Laws are rules that tell people how they should behave. When people break a law, they may be put in prison. They have to stay there for a period of time. How long depends on which law they have broken.

5

The officer stayed until a social worker came. Her name was Mrs Garvin. She asked if I had any questions about what was going on. Was I scared? Did I want a glass of water?

She was nice, but I just shook my head.
I was happy when Mum came to pick us up.

7

Mum talked on the phone almost all night. Before tucking me in, she told me Dad admitted he broke a law. He was in trouble. And he would have to stay in prison for a while.

I asked Mum if it was my fault. She said it wasn't. Dad just made a bad choice. She said no matter what, she and Dad would always love me.

My stomach didn't feel so strange after that. But why had Dad done it? He'd left us! I thought about drawing. But I was too sad to draw.

Fifty-four per cent of prisoners in the UK reported having children under the age of 18.

The next morning, I kept my head down. I tried to hide behind my books. But Kenny saw me. Kenny lives on Dad's street. He saw Dad get into the police car.

"Bailey's dad got taken away by the police last night!" Kenny yelled.

My face got hot. I crept into class, wishing I could disappear.

Later, Mr Johnson asked me a
question. I didn't even hear him.

Ava poked me in the back.
"Hey! Wake up, prisoner!"

I was so cross, I twisted around and pushed her books onto the floor.

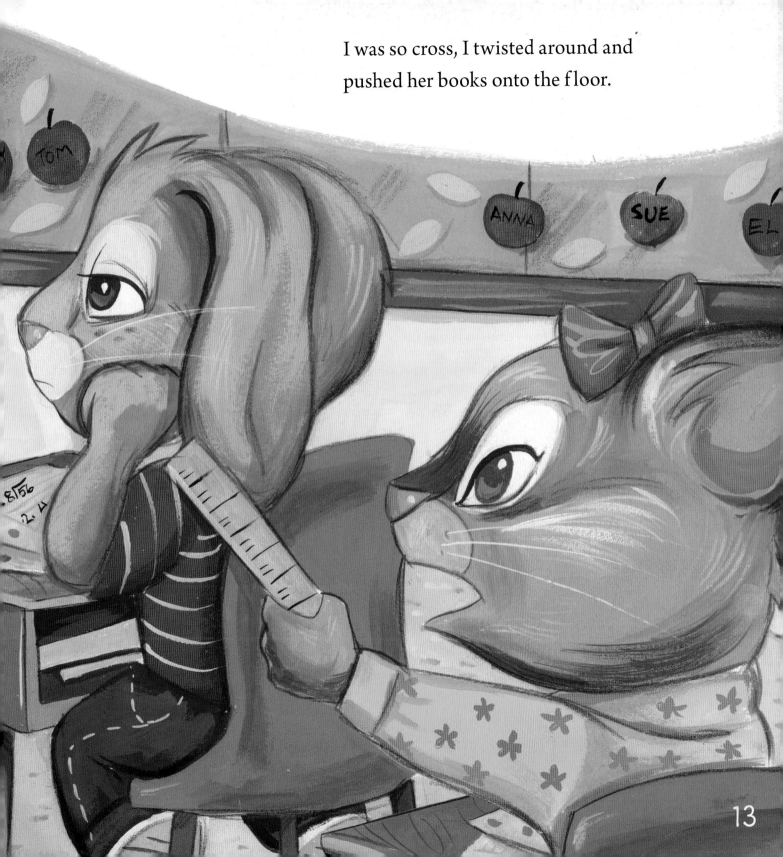

13

That's how I ended up in Miss Sanchez's office.

I'd never been in trouble before. Miss Sanchez had called my mum and found out what happened to Dad. I sat and scribbled.

"Is that a picture of you?" she asked, looking at the paper.

"I suppose so," I said. "I don't know. Everything's all messed up."

Miss Sanchez said feeling angry, sad and scared was OK. So was feeling worried and embarrassed. She gave me ideas for what to do with my "scribble" feelings. Next time, I can walk away instead of fighting. I can draw pictures or talk to someone I trust.

15

For a while, Dad was in a nearby prison. Mum visited first and told us what it was like. When we all went, we took the bus. Dad sat on the other side of a glass wall. We each talked to him on a telephone. When it was my turn, I couldn't look at him.

"I messed up, Sketch," Dad said. "What I did caused a lot of problems, and I'm sorry. I hope you'll forgive me."

I wasn't sure what to say. I just nodded.

Lots of children don't know what to say to their parent in prison. Talking about school and everyday life is a great place to start.

After four months, Dad was sent to a prison further away. The bus took all morning. When we arrived, we walked through a metal detector. The prison was really scary, but we could visit Dad without a wall between us.

It's common to feel excited, nervous and restless before and after visiting a parent in prison.

Hugging him was one of the best feelings I'd had in a long time.

19

We see Dad about once a month. In between visits, I send him drawings, and he writes me letters. Sometimes we talk on the phone.

Miss Sanchez found a group of other children who have a mum or dad in prison. We get together every Tuesday. They're cool. They understand what I'm going through.

Things have changed since Dad went to prison. Mum works even more than she used to. Grandma helps take care of us now. Mrs Garvin, the social worker, found me a mentor too. He's not my dad, but it's nice having someone to hang out with.

Staying in touch with a parent in prison helps children get used to being apart. And it helps Dad or Mum feel more like a part of the family when he or she returns.

Dad's sentence is for six years. That's a long time to wait to go fishing again. I'm still a bit angry. But I'm trying to forgive my dad, because I love him.

Glossary

arrest take and hold someone who may have broken a law

mentor person who guides or teaches

prison enclosed space where people are sent after they've been found guilty of a crime

sentence amount of time a person is required by the court to stay in a prison

social worker person trained to help people during times of trouble

Read more

Angry (Dealing with Feeling...), Isabel Thomas (Raintree, 2014)

Being Responsible (Citizenship), Cassie Mayer (Raintree, 2008)

When Dad Went Away, Liz Weir (Frances Lincoln Children's Books, 2012)

Website

www.familylives.org.uk/advice/your-family/ parenting/how-to-cope-if-a-parent-goes-to- prison/

The imprisonment of a loved one can be very overwhelming for children. It can bring about big changes and transitions.

Index

Look out for all the books in the Life's Challenges series:

Goodbye, Jeepers

The Night Dad Went to Prison

Saying Goodbye to Uncle Joe

Weekends with Dad

Raintree is an imprint of Capstone Global Library Limited, a company incorporated in England and Wales having its registered office at 264 Banbury Road, Oxford, OX2 7DY – Registered company number: 6695582

www.raintree.co.uk
myorders@raintree.co.uk

Text © Capstone Global Library Limited 2016
The moral rights of the proprietor have been asserted.

All rights reserved. No part of this publication may be reproduced in any form or by any means (including photocopying or storing it in any medium by electronic means and whether or not transiently or incidentally to some other use of this publication) without the written permission of the copyright owner, except in accordance with the provisions of the Copyright, Designs and Patents Act 1988 or under the terms of a licence issued by the Copyright Licensing Agency, Saffron House, 6–10 Kirby Street, London EC1N 8TS (www.cla.co.uk). Applications for the copyright owner's written permission should be addressed to the publisher.

Editor: Jill Kalz
Designer: Alison Thiele
Art Director: Nathan Gassman
Production Specialist: Sarah Bennett
The illustrations in this book were created with gouache and coloured pencil.

ISBN 978 1 4747 2470 8
20 19 18 17 16
10 9 8 7 6 5 4 3 2 1

British Library Cataloguing in Publication Data
A full catalogue record for this book is available from the British Library.

Acknowledgements
Thanks to our advisers for their expertise, research, and advice:

Michele Goyette-Ewing, PhD Director of Psychology Training Yale Child Study Center

Terry Flaherty, PhD Professor of English Minnesota State University, Mankato

Every effort has been made to contact copyright holders of material reproduced in this book. Any omissions will be rectified in subsequent printings if notice is given to the publisher.

All the internet addresses (URLs) given in this book were valid at the time of going to press. However, due to the dynamic nature of the internet, some addresses may have changed, or sites may have changed or ceased to exist since publication. While the author and publisher regret any inconvenience this may cause readers, no responsibility for any such changes can be accepted by either the author or the publisher.

Made in China